Ps 2:8

To Larry,
Your Spirit
shines forth as a witness for
Jesus.
God bless you & thank you
for your friendship

Joann Seleman

PATHWAY
of
Prayer Walking

~~~

Joann Tallman

WestBow
PRESS

Copyright © 2010 Joann Tallman

All rights reserved. No part of this book may be used or reproduced by any means, graphic, electronic, or mechanical, including photocopying, recording, taping or by any information storage retrieval system without the written permission of the publisher except in the case of brief quotations embodied in critical articles and reviews.

Scripture verses taken from The New King James Bible and New American Standard Bible.

WestBow Press books may be ordered through booksellers or by contacting:

WestBow Press
A Division of Thomas Nelson
1663 Liberty Drive
Bloomington, IN 47403
www.westbowpress.com
1-(866) 928-1240

Because of the dynamic nature of the Internet, any Web addresses or links contained in this book may have changed since publication and may no longer be valid. The views expressed in this work are solely those of the author and do not necessarily reflect the views of the publisher, and the publisher hereby disclaims any responsibility for them.

ISBN: 978-1-4497-0183-3 (sc)

Library of Congress Control Number: 2010926336

Printed in the United States of America

WestBow Press rev. date: 6/4/2010

Acknowledgments

Thanks to the Lord Jesus Christ for teaching me about prayer walking and leading me through so many countries to pray over the lands. Special thanks to my friends who encouraged me to write of my experiences and what the Lord has taught me. Special thanks to Vicki Williams for drawing my cover – it is exactly what I asked for. Special thanks to my "readers" who read, critiqued and gave me suggestions as I wrote these chapters.

May God be glorified and blessed in all that is written herein.

Contents

1. Acknowledgments — v
2. In the Beginning — 1
3. Prayer Walking Defined — 3
4. Victory Over the Enemy — 21
5. Prayer Walking Method — 27
6. Practical Steps — 37
7. Prayer Journey: *Teams and Team Leaders* — 43
8. Recognizing Strongholds — 47
9. Stronghold Examples — 53
10. Praise Praying — 67
11. Stronghold Chart — 73

1

In the Beginning

Every time I bow my head or my knees, and every time I open my hands in surrender or raise my arms in praise, I begin a journey along the pathway of prayer. When I whisper the name of Jesus or cry out for Abba I begin a journey along the pathway of prayer. It matters not if I kneel quietly at the altar, or sit snuggled in my prayer chair at home, when I begin a journey along the pathway of prayer.

I may begin a journey on foot in a busy city or along a deserted dirt road in the country, but when I begin in Jesus' name I am beginning a journey along the pathway of prayer. My physical position or geographical location does not matter; what matters is the condition of my heart. Am I surrendered, am I willing and humble?

Have I laid down my agenda and asked the Lord for His will? Am I prepared to pray requests and give praise rather than tell Him how I want Him to answer my requests, needs and desires?

Am I willing to talk with the Lord about my prayer needs and then leave them with Him to answer in the way that He knows is best? Am I humble enough to trust Him with the perfect answer rather than to tell Him what to do about my request? Am I surrendered, willing and humble enough to let Him tell me how and what to pray?

Oh Lord, cleanse my heart and mind. Use Your Spirit to reveal my thoughts, motives, wants and desires. Help me to recognize and turn from my pride. Help me to accept with praise and thanksgiving Your will, not mine. Remind me that You alone know my heart.

Jeremiah 17:9-10: "The heart is deceitful above all things, and desperately wicked; who can know it? I, the Lord, search the heart, I test the mind. Even to give every man according to his ways."

2

Prayer Walking Defined

Prayer walking is simply praying and walking. I have prayer walked since the mid 1970's in South Korea, France, Zimbabwe, Bophuthatswana, Africa, Kazakhstan, India, Israel, Germany and many cities in America.

I learned to prayer walk by experience. In the early years, I didn't realize that I was prayer walking but I knew that I liked to be outdoors. I enjoyed praying and praising the Lord while walking and I wanted to pray for my neighborhood.

When we lived in Harare, Zimbabwe (known as Salisbury, Rhodesia at that time) I made a conscious effort to go prayer walking. I am a morning person so I would get up early in the morning and go out to walk and pray. During the years we lived in Harare there was active civil war going on. Terrorists were in town on occasion so I learned not to walk the same pattern daily. I would walk through different neighborhoods and use different streets so naturally I would find different needs to pray about.

I learned quickly that the Holy Spirit would give me insight for areas that needed special prayer. It was a wonderful learning experience. I loved living in Harare and was not fearful, but I was cautious and used common sense. The Lord used that time to help me learn to listen carefully to His voice and to obey Him immediately if He told me to turn around or go a different way.

I recall the morning when I was walking several blocks from my home. There was a tall hedge of bushes on my left. I was walking on the sidewalk and the Holy Spirit instructed me to get away from the hedge and walk on the street. I did not question Him and immediately obeyed His instruction.

Later I asked the Lord, "Why did I need to move away from the hedge?" He helped me to understand that this was first a lesson in listening, then it was a lesson in obedience and third it was safer to be at the edge of the street. Anyone could have been hiding in the hedge with intent to harm me.

That lesson was again used in 1994 in Almaty, Kazakhstan. I was walking on Awazava Street, a main street that I walked often, but one day as I was on the sidewalk the Holy Spirit spoke to me and reminded me of my lesson in Africa. There was a tall hedge bordering the sidewalk where I was walking so I moved away from the hedge and went on my way praising the Lord. I do not know why He reminded me of the potential danger of walking close to a thick hedge but He did, and so I moved away from any potential danger.

When prayer walking, listen carefully to anything the Holy Spirit says and be instantly obedient. It may be for your safety or instruction in how to pray for a person or for a location.

In Africa, most of the time I walked alone but there came a time when a new missionary moved into my neighborhood and she would walk with me. I began to understand the power and effectiveness of two people agreeing together in prayer for a country, city and neighborhood. I know that the Biblical example of sending people out to minister in Jesus' name tells us they went two by two. But if the Lord asks you to go alone, do not be fearful, just obey. He never leaves us, so we are always walking with Him as we go out to pray over our neighborhoods or to intercede for a particular situation. Ideally, however, two people who are united in purpose, belief and spirit should prayer walk together.

Preparation is necessary prior to prayer walking. When we get ready to go prayer walking, we need to make sure that our heart is in right relation with the Lord. If we hold pride, unforgiveness or any sin in our heart, we will see very little victory in our prayers. Psalm 139:23-24 says, "Search me, O God, and know my heart; try me, and know my anxieties; and see if there is any wicked way in me, and lead me in the way everlasting."

When we prayer walk, we are out of a controlled or protected environment. The Holy Spirit is with us of course, but we are without the support of other Christians in a closed, safe environment like a prayer group.

Humility is the basis for having a prepared heart. One of the keys the Lord looks for in us as we pray is the surrender of ourselves. Surrender means what I want to do is not as important as spending time with Jesus.

One Wednesday morning in 1997 while living in Almaty, Kazakhstan, the Lord impressed on me how He wanted the day to be used. But, I already had a plan. Each Wednesday a Russian lady came to my home; we spent time in prayer and Bible study. I was guiding her through a post-abortion study.

When she arrived at my home that morning, I told her what the Lord had put in my heart. We were to sit quietly, praise Him and wait on Him. Normally we would have tea as we sat around the table studying the Bible, pray, and then visit.

But not this day. So we went to the living room and sat down. I said a simple prayer just to prepare our hearts and then we waited. Suddenly she began to cry and pray for her unsaved husband. Together we began to pray deep interceding prayer for him. We prayed and then were released to praise the Lord for what He was doing in not only her husband but also in their family. They had discussed divorce and so we also asked the Lord to reunite this family in Him.

Finally, we sensed we were finished praying and I thought we would go on with our Bible study. I went to the kitchen to put on the tea kettle and was astonished to see it was after 1:00pm in the afternoon. We had been in prayer for several hours, but it seemed like a very short time.

She rushed out to go home to her children who were coming back from school. A few days later she called to say that her husband had gone to church with her and accepted Jesus into his life. Soon after that he began to study the Word, they committed their marriage and lives to the Lord and he began to serve and grow in their church.

Would this have happened if we had not been obedient to God's instruction for changing our agenda that Wednesday? I really don't know the answer, but I do know that we were greatly blessed as we witnessed the Lord's answer to our prayers. Flexibility and obedience must go along with humility as we bow our own will and agenda to the Lord's purpose and will.

Humility is the key to an open heart. Second Chronicles 7:14 states that "**If** my people who are called by My name will humble themselves, and pray and seek My face, and turn from their wicked ways, **then** I will hear from heaven, and will forgive their sin and heal their land." *(emphasis mine)*

Most Scripture promises are conditional, the condition being that we walk in submission and obedience to the Scripture, including attitudes, thoughts and meditations. Note the conditions given in this Scripture.

(a) *If those who are called by My name*
This would be someone openly known as one who loves and serves the Lord.

(b) *will humble themselves*
It does not say to ask Him to humble us, it says to humble ourselves. That means gaining control over our carnal desires and self-importance and submitting all thoughts, desires and plans to Him.

(c) *and pray and seek My face*
This is about spending time with the Lord, getting to know Him, His Word and listening to Him.

(d) *and turn from their wicked ways*
This means walking in obedience to what He has spoken to us through the Word and through the still small voice of His Spirit within. It also means we have a choice. We must decide and choose to quit the seen and the unseen sin. Heart sin, gossip, hate, bitterness, lust, secret desires, etc., are hidden sins to people around us but not to God.

Now note the promise in this Scripture:

(e) **then** (emphasis mine) *I will hear from heaven, and will forgive their sin and heal their land.*
He, the Lord God, will hear our cries, He will forgive our individual and corporate sin then He will heal our land. What a wonderful promise for walking in obedience to His Word!

Another preparation before prayer walking is to put on the armor (protection) that Christ gave us in Ephesians 6:14-17. "Stand therefore, having girded your waist with truth, having put on the breastplate of righteousness, and having shod your feet with the preparation of the gospel of peace; above all, taking the shield of faith with which you will be able to quench all the fiery darts of the wicked one. And take the helmet of salvation, and the sword of the Spirit, which is the word of God; praying always with all prayer and supplication in the Spirit, being watchful to this end with all perseverance and supplication for all the saints."

We have to be covered and protected before we go into enemy territory. Relate your prayer walking preparation to the preparation that soldiers must make prior to going to war. They are trained to recognize the enemy and how to combat the enemy. They are given special clothes to wear. They are assigned to a leader and are expected to obey their leader's instructions.

The Lord has given us the same opportunity teaching us how to prayer walk. Paul wrote the book of Ephesians to the Christian church in Ephesus. He told them to put on the armor of God. Paul knew that Christians needed protection, physically and spiritually, from the enemy. He told them to depend upon their leader and be strong because of His might. This involves knowing what He teaches us and walking confidently in the knowledge He gives us. Ephesians 6:10 instructs, "Finally my brethren, be strong in the Lord and in the power of His might."

Paul says to put on the armor He has given us so that we are protected from the hidden agenda of the enemy. "Put on the whole armor of God, that you may be able to stand against the wiles of the devil." (Ephesians 6:11) Paul identifies for us who our enemy is. He wants us to recognize the enemy and not be taken by surprise. "For we do not wrestle against flesh and blood, but against principalities, against powers, against the rulers of the darkness of this age, against spiritual hosts of wickedness in the heavenly places." (Ephesians 6:12)

Next, Paul asks for a commitment. He suggests that we make a thought-out decision prior to the battle to walk in obedience to what we are taught and told, and to stand strong knowing that we are not fighting in our own strength but in the Lord's strength and authority. "Therefore take up the whole armor of God, that you may be able to withstand in the evil day, and having done all, to stand." (Ephesians 6:13)

Paul identifies how we are to clothe ourselves for protection. He mentions more than once "to stand". He is saying to make a commitment and then keep it. Keep yourself reminded that you are under the authority of Jesus Christ the Son of God, the Commander and Chief of the Army of God. "Stand therefore, having girded your waist with truth, having put on the breastplate of righteousness, and having shod your feet with the preparation of the gospel of peace; above all, taking the shield of faith with which you will be able to quench all the fiery darts of the wicked one. And take the helmet of salvation, and the sword of the Spirit, which is the word of God;" (Ephesians 6:14-17)

Paul reminds us to continue communication with our leader. We cannot go out in our own strength or without continuing instruction as we enter the battle field. The Holy Spirit will continue to instruct and guide us but we must be willing to listen and obey. "...praying always with all prayer and supplication in the Spirit, being watchful to this end with all perseverance and supplication for all the saints." (Ephesians 6:18)

We note that in the Ephesians reference there is not a piece of armor for our back. But God did not leave us vulnerable to the enemy. Isaiah 52:12b states "...For the Lord will go before you, and the God of Israel will be your rear guard." And in Isaiah 58:8b, "The glory of the Lord shall be your rear guard."

Exodus 14:19 says, "And the Angel of God, who went before

the camp of Israel, moved and went behind them; and the pillar of cloud went from before them and stood behind them."

These Scriptures tell us that God Himself is our rear guard. Because God has already said that He is our rear guard, we thank Him for being that protection for us. We believe in our hearts that what He says, He means. We do not have to beg or plead with Him for things He has already provided. We walk in obedience to His direction and we thank Him for His provision.

Second Corinthians 10:3 says, "For though we walk in the flesh, we do not war according to the flesh." God tells us a fact that we need to be aware of, but it is a fact bathed in encouragement. He is emphasizing to us that we are human, fleshly beings and we have limits living as humans; but our ability to succeed in following Christ is not based on human limitations.

Second Corinthians 10:4 reminds us that "the weapons of our warfare are not carnal (of the flesh) but mighty in God for pulling down strongholds..." One of the purposes of prayer walking is to break the strongholds of the enemy over an area. What is our weapon? The Word of God.

When we know, believe and call out God's Word, we use the authority He has given to us. Second Corinthians 10:5 says, "Casting down arguments and every high thing that exalts itself against the knowledge of God, bringing every thought into captivity to the obedience of Christ."

Because of the promise given to us in verse five, we recognize and cast down arguments (division) and every high (lofty) thing (thought) that exalts itself against the knowledge of God (pride, false religions, self), bringing every thought into captivity to the obedience of Christ. We humbly ask the Holy Spirit how to pray, we listen for His reply and then pray specifically against particular strongholds and bondages as He directs.

In Luke 10:19 Jesus said, "Behold, I give you the authority to trample on serpents and scorpions, and over **all** the power of the enemy, and nothing shall by any means hurt you." *(emphasis mine)* He gives us His authority. We must know and believe His Word to understand what that authority includes. He says we have authority over all the power of the enemy. That leaves us nothing to fear. All situations and circumstances are under His control. As long as His Spirit lives in us, we have the authority to bring down the enemy and we have authority over all enemy attacks.

Luke 10:19 goes on to say, "and nothing shall by any means hurt you." The hurt Jesus is talking about is all-inclusive. The Greek word, *adikeo* includes social or criminal injustice, mistreatment of any kind, legal offense, inflicting hurt or general wrongdoing. He said nothing shall hurt us. He did not say nothing would come against us. Circumstances or situations will occur which cause us pain and hurt, but He tells us those circumstances will not cause eternal or permanent harm. He will take care of any and all circumstances which come against us in the way He knows is most beneficial for us.

There are times when the Lord intervenes when we do not know we need help at that moment. Years ago my husband and I, along with our baby, were driving through the country on a small two lane road. Ditches on each side of the road and up and down hills prevented us from knowing what was ahead. Suddenly the Holy Spirit told me there was a herd of cattle in the road over the next hill. I quickly told my husband, and he slowed as we crested the hill. Sure enough there in the road was a herd of cattle milling around. They were no more aware of the danger than we had been, but because the Lord is faithful He warned us so we were not harmed nor were the cattle.

Romans 12:19 states, "Beloved, do not avenge yourselves, but rather give place to wrath; for it is written, Vengeance is Mine, I will repay," says the Lord. Webster defines vengeance as "punishment in retaliation for an injury or offense."

In 1994 as I prepared to go to Kazakhstan, I had made arrangements with a Christian missionary in Almaty to meet me at the airport, find me an apartment to rent, to get my city registration visa and to have my Kazakhstan visa extended.

Upon arrival at the Almaty airport there was no one to meet me. I had only two phone numbers of people in Almaty so I called one of them. They, along with some other people the Lord provided, got me to the apartment of the couple I had hired to help me. The man had neglected to fulfill our arrangement and he and his family were preparing to leave the country in just a few hours.

I had no place to live, no idea how to get city registration or how to extend my visa. I had been up for two days and was operating on adrenaline only. The man said I could rent their apartment while they were out of the country, so I had a place to stay at least. I sat down in a chair and went fast asleep. When I woke up, they were gone and I was alone in the apartment. I had no idea where the keys were or what to do. Then, as I looked through my things I could not find my passport. Fear began to grip me and I fought to remain calm.

I told the Lord that it was up to Him to fill in the gap, and tried not to be angry for being abandoned like this. I asked the Lord to give me His grace and peace and guidance. The next morning the phone rang, and it was the man. He told me where the house keys were and then told me he had given my passport to someone to get my city registration and extend my entry visa. I had prepaid for all these services so I would owe no more money.

I did not know who had my passport or how to get in touch with him. Through the next couple of weeks all I could do was pray. One day a knock came on my door and it was a Kazakh man with my passport. He showed it to me, but there was still no visa or registration. He asked me for $300 US. I told him that I had already paid.

He had the money to pay for the registration and visa, but wanted me to pay him another $300 to take care of this for me. I repeated (he spoke English) that I had already paid for this service. He became very angry and walked away with my passport when I refused to pay his bribe.

The day after my entry visa expired (meaning that I was in the country illegally) he returned, and when I opened the door he threw my passport into the apartment and stormed off. That night I prayed and prayed, asking the Lord what I was to do. He directed me to Luke 12:11-12, "Now when they bring you to the synagogues and magistrates and authorities, do not worry about how or what you should answer, or what you should say. For the Holy Spirit will teach you in that very hour what you ought to say."

Peace consumed me and I knew it was going to be all right. The next day I went to the government immigration office to straighten it out. The officials asked me questions, and I answered honestly and politely. When it was all said and done, they gave me a one year business multi-entry visa for Kazakhstan, my city registration and sent me on my way. They were very kind and understanding and apologized that I had been treated this way.

The Lord had prepared the way ahead of me, and He had taken care of a situation that could have been extremely difficult. But He gave me His Word and He kept it. I praise Him for being my caretaker. As He says in Zechariah 4:6, "...Not by might nor by power, but by My Spirit, says the Lord of hosts."

He will be our defense when we need defending. So His promise in Luke 10:19 that "nothing shall by any means hurt you" is accomplished by Him when we humble ourselves and allow Jesus to be our defender.

Before I go out prayer walking I often read Joshua 1:3-9. When I read those verses, I apply those scriptures personally to me. I read them as though the Lord is sending me out and has given me the land. Find Scriptures that the Lord gives to you personally and walk in the authority of those Scriptures.

Another result of prayer walking is that the Lord prepares the hearts and lives of people we may never meet. As we pray over areas, buildings and individuals along our walk, the Holy Spirit makes contact with people. I don't have a clue how this happens but I don't have to question it happening, because I have personally experienced this.

In Kazakhstan during 1995, I was continuing my prayer walks with great expectations. One day my phone rang and a male voice on the other end asked if I was Joann Tallman. When I said yes, he introduced himself as a government official and asked me to come to him for a meeting. He gave me no explanation of why. I simply said okay, and we made the necessary arrangements.

I went to that appointment with expectation that the Lord was doing something special. This man turned out to be a very influential government person from the old USSR days. He asked me about HHI and what I did in Kazakhstan. (Of course he already knew all the answers.) He then told me about a woman who needed medical help. She had been born with a heart defect about 36 years earlier, and the medical system in that area had not been able to help her. She was now close to the end of her life if there was not intervention from another source. He explained the medical problem and asked me if I would help.

I was totally unprepared for this to be the reason for the meeting. I asked him why he had called me and how did he even know about me or HHI. He smiled and said he had "heard" of the work I was doing there. He was very polite and spoke perfect English.

I told him I would have to pray about God's will for me to become involved. Then I told him that if and when the Lord confirmed that this was His will I would begin to work on the problem. I asked him to make arrangements for me to meet with the woman. Within a couple of days I was at her apartment having tea. Amira (not her real name) was a beautiful woman, soft spoken and appreciative of my time. She told me her history.

Amira was born into an Islamic Kazakh family. Both her parents had died but she had two sisters in Almaty. She told me about her medical history and the hopelessness of her case. Her long-time doctor had recently told her to go home to die because there was nothing more he could do to help her.

By this time I knew the Lord had given me permission to become involved in this situation. I explained to Amira that I would need to get to America and begin making contacts.

Upon my return to Nashville, I contacted the three major heart units we have here. No one was able to say they would care for her without full cost. Naturally she was poor and I could not afford to pay full cost for her to come here and then have open heart surgery.

I then learned of a doctor in the Memphis area who performed surgery on children from other countries. I made contact with him and explained the situation and the defect. This type of heart defect is not uncommon and is normally corrected soon after birth on babies born in the United States. Even though Amira was in her mid-thirties he agreed to look at her medical records.

After her paperwork was translated into English, I faxed everything to the doctor and he studied her records. I went to

Memphis and met with him. He explained the procedure and said that he felt it was worth a try. Amira was still healthy enough and strong enough to withstand open heart surgery.

I called her and we began to work on transportation for Amira and her sister to fly to Nashville. After they arrived and rested for a few days we left for Memphis. Again, the Lord used many people during this time to fill the needs and bring this young woman here.

The day came for her surgery. The next morning they let her sister and me go into ICU to visit her. Amira was sleepy but awake. She was pale and she hurt but she knew she would live. The doctor gave us a great report. He said the surgery went easily and the repair was quick. There was not one complication or delay.

I notified the prayer team in Nashville, knowing that the Lord had once again intervened and blessed this dear woman and answered our prayers for her life, her healing and her future. After a couple of weeks I was able to return Amira to my home in Nashville. She rested and had a final check up with the doctor in Memphis and prepared for her return to Almaty.

Several Sundays while they were with me both she and her sister attended church with me. After church the last Sunday she was with me, we ate lunch and went sightseeing. Mid-afternoon she asked if we were going to church that night. I told her if she felt up to it, yes we would go. She said she wanted to go.

That evening when the invitation was given for ones to accept

Jesus as their Savior, Amira bolted out of the pew and literally ran to the altar. I followed, absolutely amazed, and held her as she spoke with the pastor and prayed for Jesus to come into her life. Her countenance changed, she had joy, a smile, and a light in her eyes that had not been there previously. She was born again and she knew it.

The next day I drove back home after taking Amira and her sister to the airport to return to Kazakhstan. I reflected on the steps that were necessary to bring her into the Kingdom of God. Did it begin with a prayer walk? Did it begin with claiming victory over the government buildings in Almaty? I believe it did. I believe when we prayer walk it opens opportunities for the Holy Spirit to do His work in the lives and journeys of many people.

3

Victory Over the Enemy

The Scripture is very clear that we have an enemy waiting to bring destruction and defeat to us in any way he can. When we begin to do anything for the enlargement and advancement of God's kingdom the enemy begins to fight us. Jesus Himself warns us so we are not taken off guard.

In John 10:10 Jesus says, "The thief does not come except to steal, and to kill, and to destroy. I have come that they may have life, and that they may have it more abundantly." Scripture gives us the truth, saying we will not be defeated but that we will be granted victory through the power of His Spirit in us and Him working in our circumstances.

Revelation 12:11 says, "And they overcame him (Satan) by the blood of the Lamb and by the word of their testimony, and they did not love their lives to the death."

Isaiah 54:17 reminds us that "No weapon formed against you shall prosper, and every tongue which rises against you in judgment you shall condemn. This is the heritage of the servants of the Lord, and their righteousness is from Me," says the Lord." There is life, health and victory in God's Word but we must learn to use it appropriately and effectively. When the enemy comes to kill, steal and destroy we have the authority from Jesus Christ, the Son of God, to take authority over him.

Again, in Luke 10:19, "Behold, I give you the authority to trample on serpents and scorpions, and over all the power of the enemy, and nothing shall by any means hurt you." Speak that verse out loud when temptation, fear or deception come against you. Remember that Jesus said we can bind up the enemy in His name and let the Father deal with him.

Matthew 18:18 promises, "Assuredly, I say to you, whatever you bind on earth will be bound in heaven, and whatever you loose on earth will be loosed in heaven." Bind the enemy that comes against you in Jesus' name and send him back to the Father for Him to deal with. Then go forth singing praise to Jesus for the victory He gives you.

Remember that victory may be a process and not an instant miracle. But we have Hebrews 11:1 to hold onto for the victorious freedom that comes only from the Lord: "Now faith is the substance of things hoped for, the evidence of things not seen." If God's Word says it, then we can believe it and go forth with joy in believing He has heard us and is working all things out for our good.

Romans 8:28 promises us, "And we know that all things work together for good to those who love God, to those who are the called according to His purpose." We must make sure we are humble and our heart is surrendered to the Lord, then we will have the confidence that He is able to fulfill His Word for us.

When I was about eight years old, the Holy Spirit spoke to me one Sunday night and said, "You will serve Me on the foreign mission field." I was too young to fully understand all that meant but as I grew up I never lost sight of the secret words He had spoken to me. My Mom prayed and prayed for me, knowing that the Lord had a call on my life.

In 1975 the Lord renewed that call on my life and set in motion the journey that was ahead. Now after all these years I know the reality of Job 42:2. "The purpose of God can not be thwarted." No matter how young or inexperienced we are, God will fulfill His purpose for our lives when we surrender to Him. The old saying that God does not call the prepared, He prepares the called, is so true.

He did not expect me to know how to go alone as a missionary to Central Asia. He took me step by step, taught me and prepared me. He opened doors and led me in fulfilling His desired purpose. But first I had to surrender all my desires, plans and will to Him and His purpose.

Divorce after twenty-two years of marriage left me totally confused but the Lord used that to teach me about my own pride, selfishness and self-will. After divorce at forty years old I thought the Lord would never use me again but oh, how wrong I was about Him. He is a gentle, loving God of healing and restoration. He rebuilt my life bringing purpose to me and honor to Himself. As it says in Romans 8:31, "What then shall we say to these things? If God is for us, who can be against us?"

Our confidence is in God's faithfulness to fulfill His Word. It is not in ourselves or in how much we know. God promises us that His Word is sure and steady. Isaiah 55:11 promises, "So shall My Word be that goes forth from My mouth; it shall not return to Me void, but it shall accomplish what I please, and it shall prosper in the thing for which I sent it."

One day in Almaty, Kazakhstan I prepared to go out prayer walking. I left my flat and was almost to the street when the Holy Spirit alerted me to some type of danger. I stopped and looked around. Across the street diagonally was a man looking at me. He started to cross the street towards me. The man held something dark in both hands close to his mid-section and never took his eyes off me.

The Lord said *walk away*. I started to walk quickly and the man sped up. He was coming across to my sidewalk and coming towards me very quickly. Suddenly I knew what to do.

This was a very busy street. It had an electric train in the middle, plus cars zooming by, but suddenly the Lord gave me clarity. I walked quickly to the middle of the street between the train tracks and in the middle of the cars going both ways. Then I stood there. The man could not come close to me, or many people would see what he intended.

He stood on the sidewalk and watched as I ran between cars and got to the other side of the street. Safe and out of his sight I quickly made my way to the next main street and the bus stop. I gave the Lord praise for His idea because it certainly proved to be a great strategy, even if it was strange, for keeping me safe.

"The name of the Lord is a strong tower, the righteous (in Jesus) run into it and are safe." (Proverbs 18:10) I use this verse so very often. The enemy not only tries to keep us from accepting Jesus as our Savior, he tries to bring discouragement and defeat to us once we have accepted Him.

Amira, the dear friend I told you about in Chapter 2 who came to Nashville from Almaty for open heart surgery had to return home without anyone to disciple her or stand with her as she transcended from Islam to Christianity. The Lord gave us community, but we have an obligation to reach out to find that community and the community has an obligation to find those who need them.

Amira had not reached out to anyone, and those I had contacted had not reached out to her either. So when I returned to Kazakhstan she was living in defeat and discouragement and was once again experiencing heart problems.

I went to visit Amira as soon as I arrived. She looked awful. She was short of breath and pale. She was going downhill and she knew it. Amira began to explain to me what had happened. I had given her a Bible, but she had not read it. She had not told her family about her decision to follow Jesus because they were practicing Muslims and they would not have accepted her choice to follow Jesus.

Most Christians have no idea how difficult it is to deal with the persecution that comes when people leave a cult or a false religion to follow Jesus. We have had a paved road with very few road blocks and yet our commitment to Christ is very shallow. As we sat and talked that day I explained to Amira about spiritual warfare and the victory we have in Christ. We read the Scriptures and she began to understand the faithfulness of our Lord.

I explained that her healing was not temporary and while Satan could mask her healing and give her symptoms, he could not undo what God had done. We read and talked, and then began to pray in Jesus' name.

As I prayed, Amira's physical body began to strengthen, her face began to show life and light once again. I believe she grasped the true victory of Jesus and what He had done for her in redeeming her and healing her.

That was the last time Satan had victory in her body. Amira strengthened and grew, and today is a strong, healthy woman. Only God could have worked this out. Only the blood of Jesus and His Word could have brought the victory to her for not only this life but for eternity as well.

Praise God for caring so much for one woman. And He cares for each individual who could easily be overlooked and missed. Amira could have died but the Lord put in place a long journey in order for her to come to the full understanding of Jesus' destiny for her.

4

Prayer Walking Method

What comes to mind when you hear the terms "prayer walking" and "prayer journey?" My personal definitions are these: prayer walking is in a smaller area like a neighborhood or city and is done consistently; while a prayer journey takes several days or longer, covers many miles and is a specifically planned trip.

If we are prayer walking within a city, the Lord may ask us to cover a different area each week or every few days. As an example, if you walk to work you may cover the same area everyday about the same time. When you are listening to the Lord and praying over an area, that is prayer walking. Use this time to break strongholds and to call on the Holy Spirit.

When I am in another country to prayer walk, I have a set time to go out. I set aside specific hours and days each week. Naturally every time I go to the market or I go for an appointment, I use that time to prayer walk also.

Several years ago when I worked a regular job each day, I parked my car in the same place about two blocks from my office. As I walked across the same path day after day I used that time to pray over the office complex. I would call down the strongholds and replace them with particular gifts or fruits of the Holy Spirit. As the Lord revealed the strongholds of the area, I would name them and bind them in the name of Jesus Christ. I would name one of the characteristics of Christ or fruits of the Holy Spirit and ask the Holy Spirit to replace those which had been bound with a specific fruit, gift or characteristic of the Holy Spirit.

Matthew 12:43-45 says, "When an unclean spirit goes out of a man, he goes through dry places, seeking rest, and finds none. Then he says, 'I will return to my house from which I came.' And when he comes, he finds it empty, swept, and put in order. Then he goes and takes with him seven other spirits more wicked than himself, and they enter and dwell there; and the last state of that man is worse than the first."

It is very important to always fill the emptiness left by the removal of the evil with the Holy Spirit. For example, if I am in an area where the Lord has said there is a spirit of anger, I come against that by using the fruits of the spirit from Galatians 5:22-23. "But the fruit of the Spirit is love, joy, peace, longsuffering, kindness, goodness, faithfulness, gentleness, self-control. Against such there is no law." I replace the ungodly spirits with Godly characteristics or fruit of the Spirit.

One day as I prayer walked in Mea Sherim, the Jewish Orthodox living area of Jerusalem, Israel, I was stopped by the word "abuse" spoken to my heart from the Holy Spirit. I saw nothing except a street of dirt, beige stone apartment houses and children's toys. I stopped to listen, and heard nothing. But I knew what the Holy Spirit had said to my heart, so I began to pray against abuse of all kinds. I walked slowly and made a couple of turns praying all the time against hurt and trauma, against the emotional damage of abuse until the Holy Spirit gave me release to move on.

My heart hurt, knowing that close by someone was hiding behind a mask which portrayed that all was well, when in reality a heart was broken and the scars on that heart could not be mended without Jesus. But as I spoke out God's words of victory and healing and bound the actions of Satan in Jesus' name I knew that Jesus, their Messiah, was speaking and comforting and bringing healing to someone and possibly an entire family.

Prayer walking is not only for the people we walk by, or the geographical location; prayer walking is for us. Individually we will be ministered to and brought into a closer personal relationship with Jesus through obedience and listening to Him as we go. Prayer walking results in personal relationships with people and being able to serve others in Jesus' name.

In 1994 in Almaty I went to a store to buy eggs and milk. I stood in a long line waiting my turn to go in. When it was almost my turn they said they were out of food. I decided to walk to the bread store and see if I could get some bread.

I noticed a very small, very old lady who had been in front of me in the egg line. She turned to walk down the street. The Lord really zoomed my spiritual and physical eyes on to her. Walking slowly behind her, I followed her to the bread store. She did not stand in the line but instead backed up against the wall of the small dark bakery. She waited, but what for? I did not understand. Finally she said something, but the clerk shook her head "no" without even looking up. The little lady slowly shuffled out of the bread store.

I followed, staying close enough to see her. She turned into the little street bazaar a couple of blocks further so I went in behind her. She went kiosk to kiosk saying something. Finally one man took a small glass jar she had in her little bag and he dropped in two already broken eggs. She bowed her head to him and smiled her toothless smile and went to the next kiosk.

After another man gave her one potato, I realized she was begging. She was stopping at each kiosk asking for food. She began to walk out of the market with her broken eggs and one potato. I stepped in front of her and in my very limited Russian language asked if I could help her. She shook her head no, and started to leave. I asked her if she needed food, she responded yes, but explained that no one could give her any today.

I guided her back into the bazaar and we went kiosk to kiosk looking for the things she needed. Tea, sugar, salt, and other essentials. We picked out some fresh veggies and fresh eggs (or as fresh as they were able to be). I walked with her to her home carrying her bag of food. We did a lot of smiling, hand holding, laughing and very little talking. We arrived at her apartment and I gave her the bag at her door and went home.

I prayed all week for the Lord to let me find her at the market the next Wednesday. I went expectantly and yes, there she was. Once again we went shopping. As we walked back toward her apartment, I put my arm around her shoulders before I remembered that I had been told never to do that because it was considered rude. But, rather than her pulling away and looking at me like I was wrong, I felt her little shoulders relax and she moved a step closer to my side.

I wanted to cry right then, but waited till I had her settled in her apartment. Over and over again the Lord led me to her. Eventually I was able to give her a Bible and some clothes, including a blue sweater that I never saw her without.

I learned a valuable lesson just by allowing the Holy Spirit to give me His spiritual eyesight. I met this delightful woman, and was able to be a conduit for the Lord. In the process I was blessed more than I could ever explain. When we prayer walk we must pay attention to everyone around us, because the Lord may have a personal assignment for us that day.

I remember the first day I prayer walked in Israel. I was new there and had not made friends yet. I was renting a room in an apartment. I knew the Lord had sent me there to pray and prayer walk and wait for further directions. I went out prayer walking in my neighborhood. There were many small walking streets between buildings and I had no sense of direction inside the maze.

I walked and prayed and turned corners and crossed streets, and then decided it was time to go home. I turned around to go back the way I had come, but I was lost. I had no idea which way to go. I kept walking, saying to the Lord that I knew that *He* knew where we were, but that I could use some help at that point. I figured I would keep walking until He told me to stop.

I came to an intersection I did not recognize and stood there. I told the Lord I did not know where to go and asked Him to tell me. He gave me a heart sense to turn left, so I did. I walked and walked, and then suddenly there was a restaurant that was next door to my building.

Over and over the Lord has been faithful to direct me, whether it is for prayer instruction or simply to get me home. The key is to let Him be in control, trust that He is in control and then relax knowing that He will instruct and guide.

After you designate a committed prayer walking time, ask the Lord where He wants you to go. Use a city or county map, pray over it and ask the Lord to give you His direction for prayer walking. Keep a journal of prayer walking. Record everything the Lord speaks to you. Keep a record of Scriptures you used and what the need was in a particular area.

In any location you are going to prayer walk, you want to identify false doctrines, idolatry, strongholds or beliefs in spirits other than God. In most American cities we will find the false religions of Islam, Buddhism, animism, shamanism, idolatry, witchcraft, new age, spiritualism, humanism, Hinduism, Mormonism, Jehovah Witness, Free Masonry and the social wrongs of ethnic abuse, anti-Semitism, drugs, plus much more. We need to recognize beliefs and doctrines that are contrary to God's Word.

When we are prayer walking, we will come against identified strongholds caused by sin, false doctrines, false religions and social wrongs. The Lord will identify spiritual bondages and strongholds in geographical areas while prayer walking. When we identify the strongholds or bondages we bind them in Jesus' name and we replace them with an opposite spirit.

During 1994 I was prayer walking in Almaty. I had become aware of a very odd thing in that city. The atmosphere always seemed darkened. Even if the clouds were gone, there seemed to be a dark cloud that permeated the city. Walking home on Tole Be Street, I asked the Lord about this darkness. Why is it always dark when I look around? This was not night darkness, it was like looking through a dark glass. I also asked, why is there so much evil here?

The Lord explained to me that for many years Kazakhstan had not had His presence. The Holy Spirit had not hovered over or lived in this land that had been ruled by Communism. He reminded me that even though America had left its roots of a Biblical foundation, the Holy Spirit was still present, so the light of Christ permeated our country because there was a remnant of Christianity still living there.

He reminded me that evil abounds in darkness and darkness is fertile ground for evil to grow and reproduce. Of course then I understood that I needed to proclaim the light of Jesus in this land. I needed to bind away the darkness in Jesus' name and ask the Holy Spirit to live through the missionaries and the new believers there to bring the life and light of Jesus to Kazakhstan.

Communism was a curse over the former USSR countries, but with Christians moving into Kazakhstan to help mature the Church of Jesus Christ, the curse would bow its knee and authority to the name of Jesus. Proverbs 26:2 says, "Like a flitting sparrow, like a flying swallow, so a curse without cause shall not alight."

Galatians 3:13 reads, "Christ has redeemed us from the curse of the law, having become a curse for us..." We are free from bondages, curses and strongholds because of the sacrifice of Jesus Christ, the Lamb of God, and the Savior of all mankind.

We identify the destructive stronghold or bondage, and in the name of Jesus we plead the blood of Jesus over the area. We break the stronghold in the name of Jesus, and then we ask the Holy Spirit to replace that spirit with one of the characteristics of Christ or fruits of the Holy Spirit.

There is no fear of repercussion while out prayer walking when we are properly prepared. There is one sentence in the Lord's prayer that I use on a regular basis. Because it is Jesus' words, and He was telling the disciples to use these words, they are mine to use also. "And do not lead us (me) into temptation, but deliver us (me) from the evil one." (Matthew 6:13a)

I ask the Father to keep me from temptation and deliver me from evil and He does it. Jesus says in John 8:32, "You shall know the truth and the truth shall make you free". Through Christ we are set free from all sin, grief, sorrow, bondage and fear. We are protected from our flesh and the lies and deceptions of the enemy. Knowing God's Word gives us the faith to walk in His protection and to be able to walk for Him. Romans 10:17 teaches that "Faith comes by hearing, and hearing by the Word of God."

It is always effective to use God's Word in praying. As it says in Isaiah 55:11, "My Word will not return to Me void". He did not say that *our word* would not return void. The only permanent victory is in proclaiming *God's Word* over an area or a situation.

Use praise praying while you are prayer walking. Remember that David, under the inspiration of the Spirit of God, says in Psalm 22:3, "But You (God) are holy, enthroned in the praises of Israel." God inhabits the praises of His people. We are His people when we are in covenant with Him through the New Covenant of Jesus Christ.

Praise tells the enemy we trust in the sovereignty of God. Praise tells God we have completely given over our life to Him to use in any manner He chooses. The Hebrew word for inhabit in this verse is *yawshab*. It means "to remain."

As we praise Him for removing the strongholds and putting His Spirit in that place, we are saying that we believe it is accomplished as He said. The enemy is defeated and victory is claimed because of His Word.

5

Practical Steps

We should go prayer walking two by two if possible. We will not draw attention to ourselves that way. If we are prayer walking in an area full of idolatry or false religion we need to remain as unobtrusive as possible.

If we go out four or six at a time with big crosses hanging around our necks and Bibles under our arms, people are going to stare and then we alert a heathen or a hostile community to what we are doing. The enemy will take that opportunity to stop us. If we go by ourselves, we are not alone. He is with us, but ideally we should always have a prayer walking partner. When we prayer walk we make an effort not to draw attention to ourselves.

All of us will do things a bit differently. I do not think the Lord cares if we overdo some things. For instance, I believe in anointing with oil, so I anoint my feet and hands before leaving my home. Oil is a symbol of the Holy Spirit. It gives me a reminder of the protection and power of the Holy Spirit.

Joshua 1:3-9 says, "Every place that the sole of your foot will tread upon I have given you, as I said to Moses. From the wilderness and this Lebanon as far as the great river, the River Euphrates, all the land of the Hittites, and to the Great Sea toward the going down of the sun, shall be your territory.

"No man shall be able to stand before you all the days of your life; as I was with Moses, so I will be with you. I will not leave you nor forsake you. Be strong and of good courage, for to this people you shall divide as an inheritance the land which I swore to their fathers to give them. Only be strong and very courageous, that you may observe to do according to all the law which Moses My servant commanded you; do not turn from it to the right hand or to the left, that you may prosper wherever you go.

"This Book of the Law shall not depart from your mouth, but you shall meditate in it day and night, that you may observe to do according to all that is written in it. For then you will make your way prosperous, and then you will have good success. Have I not commanded you? Be strong and of good courage; do not be afraid, nor be dismayed, for the Lord your God is with you wherever you go."

The Lord will tell me specific strongholds that have a grip in the area I am prayer walking. I pray for every person in each home I pass. I plead the blood of Jesus over every building and home. When children are playing outside, I also plead the blood of Jesus over them and ask the Holy Spirit to save them.

When I say "plead the blood of Jesus" I mean that I speak out the power and authority of the blood of Jesus Christ. His blood shed was the final sacrifice necessary for the forgiveness of sin. There is power in the blood – think back to instructions God gave the Israelites the last night they were in Egypt. He said sacrifice a lamb and sprinkle the blood of the lamb on the doorposts of your house to keep you safe when the angel of death goes through the village. (Jesus is called the Lamb of God in John 1:29, "The next day John saw Jesus coming toward him, and said, "Behold! The Lamb of God who takes away the sin of the world!") God said, when He saw the blood of the sacrificial lamb they put on their doors He would not touch them. Exodus 12:13 says, "Now the blood shall be a sign for you on the houses where you are. And when I see the blood, I will pass over you; and the plague shall not be on you to destroy you when I strike the land of Egypt."

Pleading the blood of Jesus over an area speaks protection and provision for that area or people. Pharaoh was the enemy and was empowered by Satan's spirit with the intent to kill all the Israelites or keep them enslaved. Because of the power of the blood of the sacrifice Satan could not kill the Israelites. The same is still in effect today. The power of the blood of Jesus keeps us safe and protects us from the enemy.

One day in Almaty, I prepared to go prayer walking. I went out and walked to a familiar corner. The Holy Spirit told me to turn right. I turned right and walked about two blocks and He said to turn right again. I had never been on that street, so I turned right and walked one-half a block and He told me to stop. I looked around, wondering what this was all about.

On my right was a small butcher shop that I had never seen. I went in, stepping down one step to enter, and stood there looking around in this very small store. Nothing made me sense I was to stay, but as I prepared to leave, someone behind me said "Joann Tallman?"

I turned to see two people, a man and a woman standing behind me. They repeated, "Joann Tallman?" I answered "Yes, I am." They were both talking at once as they took my arms and walked out of the shop with me.

Their story was this. They had come from Singapore to seek information about opening a Christian-based school in Almaty. When they arrived, they met some missionaries and when the Almaty-based missionaries found out what they were doing, they recommended that these two people talk to me. But they had no idea how to get in contact with me.

That very morning this couple got up and prayed for the Lord to lead them to me. They felt inclined to take a taxi from the south part of town where they were staying to this part of town where I lived.

They asked the Holy Spirit to guide them to me. He did! They knew when to exit the taxi and which direction to walk. There in the middle of this block in a small off-side butcher shop we met. We spent the rest of the day together rejoicing, talking business and praising the Lord for His guidance and direction. Just as He led them to me, He would lead them as they investigated the possibility of opening a Christian school in Almaty.

I know prayer walking makes a difference. Ask God to place confidence in your heart that prayer walking is important. We can come against evil, crime, corruption, greed and selfishness, and He will break the strongholds.

Jesus Christ said, "He has sent Me to heal the brokenhearted, to proclaim liberty to the captives and recovery of sight to the blind, to set at liberty those who are oppressed..." (Luke 4:18). In carrying out His commission to free those held by strongholds and bondages, we can begin by preparing the spiritual atmosphere and geographical area through prayer.

Here are some specific geographical locations which can be targeted for prayer walking:
- college or university campuses
- abortion clinics and planned parenthood offices
- orphanages and day care facilities
- pensioner homes and nursing homes

Other locations where you can prayer walk are:
- hospitals and clinics
- schools
- bars
- sex shops
- areas of prostitution
- drug dealer or drug exchange locations
- government buildings, city, county and state
- buildings which house cults or false religions
- Masonic Lodges
- places where Martial Arts are taught
- prisons or jails
- churches
- homes of ministers
- local political party headquarters

- media centers for TV and radio
- malls
- entertainment centers
- universities and colleges
- areas where youth gather

Steps to take before prayer walking:
1) prepare yourself spiritually by submitting to the searching of your heart by the Holy Spirit;
2) cover yourself with the armor;
3) ask the Lord for a location;
4) remind yourself you are going in the authority of the Scriptures; and
5) know God's Word.

6

Prayer Journey:

Teams and Team Leaders

A prayer journey is when you go to a specific location for an extended period of days to prayer walk an area. It is not a vacation or something to be done on the spur of the moment. It takes much preparation, both practically and spiritually, to be ready for a prayer journey.

To begin, research the geographical location you will be prayer walking. Go to the library and look up the history associated with the area. The findings will vary according to the country and various locations within the country you are planning to prayer walk.

- Research where occult activities were held, including areas where altars for human and animal sacrifice would have been located.

- Learn about the religious practices of the country.
- Research the methods of punishment and geographical locations of jails or prisons.
- Learn about cultural practices for the area. Some will be occult and will need to be dealt with in Jesus' name.
- Research the acceptable dress code you will need in your designated country.
- Learn as much as you can about the facilities and the technologies available in your destination.
- Only healthy and strong individuals should plan an extended prayer journey.
- The "team" should meet together for several months prior to departure in order to build unity and to be in one accord.
- Each team member should have their own prayer team covering them individually during preparation months and during the prayer journey.
- Each individual's prayer team should agree to make a commitment to pray for the rest of the team also.

Each team member will have their own prayer style. By meeting together in the months before departure the team will become comfortable praying together. The comfort level comes from being together, praying together and getting to know each other prior to departure. During this time, the team leader will also set a focus and a goal for the prayer journey. Each participant must agree to work together as a team and not become individualistic.

Each team member will have time of private prayer as the journey progresses. During these private prayer times, team members need to listen carefully to the Holy Spirit as He gives clarity and direction for prayer. The team member should then share what has been given with the team leader, for permission to share it with the group.

The team leader is not to be a controlling authoritarian figure, but must be a person with good listening skills and a heart of compassion, mercy and love. The team leader must be strong but flexible, and gentle but use authority to keep the team bound together in love, unity and in focus.

Being on a prayer journey in a foreign country is exciting. It refines our listening skills and teaches us to humbly share what we hear from the Lord. Each team member must make the decision prior to departure to be submissive to the team leader. Even if a team member does not agree with every direction that the leader gives, the team member must be willing to submit to the authority of the leadership for the good of the team.

Team members must not allow themselves to become divisive. A divided team will not survive the culture change nor will the Lord be able to use them for spiritual change in their assigned location. A divided team will be defeated by Satan very quickly. A team with unsubmissive members will suffer spiritual defeat as a team; thus unity must be maintained. If the team leader needs to take strong action toward one member the others need to stand back and pray for reconciliation. If submission and reconciliation are not possible the team member must leave the team and return home.

7

Recognizing Strongholds

Many strongholds are carnal flesh in action, not demonic. Recognize the difference. Carnal weaknesses are targeted by Satan to cause us to fall. A person with a "natural" (carnal) quick temper or who becomes angry easily must choose to put that flesh/carnal quality on the altar and choose to let the Holy Spirit remove that stronghold. Satan will use that flesh/carnal quality to discourage us, hurt others and defeat our growth to maturity.

Strongholds can be identified in our thought patterns and ideas as well as our words and actions. Satan's job is to undermine our prayers and neutralize our walk with God. If we tolerate sin existing unchallenged in our life, we leave ourselves open for satanic attack. Willful disobedience to God's word (Scripture or Holy Spirit revelation) is tolerating sin.

The carnal areas in our character that we hide in darkness (do not admit or do not submit to the Holy Spirit for redemption) are areas which will cause us to fall naturally, and are the areas that Satan will target for his use in our lives. "And why do you look at the speck in your brother's eye, but do not consider the plank in your own eye? Or how can you say to your brother, 'Let me remove the speck from your eye;' and look, a plank is in your own eye? Hypocrite! First remove the plank from your own eye, and then you will see clearly to remove the speck from your brother's eye." (Matthew 7:3-5)

If we live in darkness, which is the absence of Christ's presence, revelation and the absence of the Holy Spirit emotionally, spiritually or mentally, the solution is to pray God's word into our daily life. We can then walk victoriously in believing and proclaiming His word. John 8:12 says, "Then Jesus again spoke to them, saying, I am the light of the world; he who follows Me will not walk in the darkness, but will have the light of life."

Living in darkness blinds us to truth. It draws us into the world's value system and causes us to tolerate sin; consequently we then compromise Godly values for immorality, greed and self-indulgence. When we recognize sin in our lives we need to search for the root of that sin. Sin is a symptom of walking in darkness. We lose fine tuning of the Holy Spirit when we choose to live in the world.

Another symptom of living in darkness is moral depravity. The worldly culture promotes moral depravity. We are told it is advisable to live together before marriage; it is a woman's choice to have an abortion; and that it is good to promote yourself first or think of others after you reach your goal in the career field. We live in a "me first" entitlement time and it's all sin.

In Second Corinthians 5:17 Paul tells the church at Corinth that "...if anyone is a new creation; old things have passed away; behold, all things have become new." He strongly advises the Roman Christians in his letter to them to live a Godly life. He says, "I beseech you therefore, brethren, by the mercies of God, that you present your bodies a living sacrifice, holy, acceptable to God, which is your reasonable service. And do not be conformed to this world, but be transformed by the renewing of your mind, that you may prove what is that good and acceptable and perfect will of God." (Romans 12:1-2)

Never argue with your accuser, whether Satan is speaking condemnation in your mind or people are speaking condemnation to you. Always agree that your nature is basically sinful. But remind yourself (and them) that you are blood-bought and blood-washed. Romans 8:1 says, "there is therefore now no condemnation for those in Christ Jesus." Grace and mercy have been activated on your behalf.

In Ephesians 6:12 we are told that "our struggle is not against flesh and blood, but against the rulers, against the powers, against the world forces of this darkness, against the spiritual forces of wickedness in the heavenly places."

When people bring accusations against you (whether fair or true), do not defend yourself or justify your actions or words. Let God defend you, apologize and restore yourself at once to the other person without taking or holding offense. If we release it to the Lord He will bring a just and correct solution.

When someone accuses you of hurting their feelings, being insensitive, not understanding, or being bossy or impolite, ask the

Lord to reveal any element of truth which is in that accusation. Confess it, repent, ask the Holy Spirit to fill you with the full character of Christ, cover the incident with the blood of Jesus and go forth in humility.

Usually there is an element of truth in any accusation which comes against us. It is better to humble ourselves and receive the accusation, even when over-stated or coming from over-reaction, than to argue or justify ourselves. In doing that, we learn humility and we let the Lord justify us.

Humility results in unity. Without unity the personal, city or countrywide move of the Lord will be hindered. Lack of unity is self-kingdom building, not God-kingdom building. Pride is usually the base sin for lack of unity, whether individual or corporate disunity.

Humility replaces pride. Humility may have to begin with a physical act of obedience. The "will" (soul) catches up when you make a volitional choice to act in obedience. Learn to be an offensive prayer rather than a defensive prayer. As your discernment develops, the Holy Spirit will give you insight into matters that need prayer, whether offensive or defensive. Discernment is an essential element in prayer walking. Ask the Holy Spirit to make you very sensitive to His voice and leading when you are out walking and praying for individuals, areas or strongholds.

You must always be true to Him with what He shows you through discernment. Never reveal, even for the excuse of added prayer, what He shows or tells you privately in prayer when it deals with an individual. He will stop telling you the secrets of

His heart if He can't trust you with them. If He reveals to you a community issue or particular strongholds in areas, of course make those a matter for community prayer.

One time the Lord spoke to my heart that the husband of one of my friends was having an affair. I began to pray for the Lord to intervene. My friend did not talk to me about the home situation and I did not mention anything the Lord had revealed to me.

After several weeks, one morning as I was praying the Holy Spirit urged me to drive across town to a particular restaurant. He gave me no other instructions. I did as He instructed and went into the restaurant to find my friend's husband in a booth with another woman eating a meal.

It was not my business to judge or correct, but when he saw me he knew that I knew what was happening. Why did the Lord give me that instruction? I believe it was so I would pray more fervently and with specific Scriptures. I could pray effectively for this couple and their marriage.

As it turned out, their marriage went through a very difficult time, my friend did come and talk to me, but I never told her what the Lord had revealed to me. That was not necessary. I could pray with her, listen to her and pray for their marriage to be healed. The results were up to the choices they made in obedience to the Lord's guidance.

Finally, remember that when you recognize a stronghold, never stop with only binding or rebuking it. Always pray the opposite spirit over that location, organization or person. We never want to leave an empty place to which Satan can return. We want to speak life into a situation or person by speaking God's Word or a characteristic of Christ to seal the emptiness with God's Spirit. *(See chart in Chapter 10)*

8

Stronghold Examples

• **Addictions**

Alcohol, sex, gambling, drugs, pornography, food, the need for attention, and money. All of these are idolatry.

Exodus 20:3 says, "You shall have no other gods before me." In today's society, idolatry includes addictions. People's affections are centered on the things that they crave, elevating the addiction over God.

Webster defines idol as "an object of devotion." Drugs, sex and other people can be an object of devotion. What captures your thoughts and meditations? What do you obsess over? When you read God's Word, ask the Holy Spirit to reveal to you strongholds or bondages that hold or possess you. Ask Him to show you in Scripture how He takes care of them.

- **Confusion**

Webster defines confusion as "make mentally uncertain," "jumble." Confusion is evidenced in people who constantly change their mind. They make a decision, then change that decision for another. They try one thing, and then try another with little success. First Corinthians 14:33 says, "For God is not the author of confusion, but of peace, as in all churches of the saints." Since confusion is not from Him, it can be broken. Confusion can be found in personal lives, governments, businesses and churches. We need to identify powers, principalities and spiritual powers over governments, churches or community areas that cause confusion, and pray over those strongholds for deliverance.

- **Control**

We need to begin by making sure that control is not an issue in our own lives. Each of us should do spiritual check-ups of our own motives and meditations. Be submissive and teachable when the Holy Spirit points out something that needs to be changed. We must be accountable to the people in our lives that we submit to as our spiritual authority.

Jeremiah 17:9-10 teaches that "The heart is deceitful above all things, and desperately wicked; who can know it? I, the Lord, search the heart; I test the mind, even to give every man according to his ways, according to the fruit of his doings."

Control can be evidenced in many ways. Here are just a few to consider:

- Always professing to be the most knowledgeable about a certain subject. (unteachable spirit).

- Constantly telling others what to do, without having the positional authority.
- Talking excessively loud.
- Consistently demanding to be first in line, first to tell a story or incident, or first in everything you do.
- Often judging others as wrong or stupid.
- Not being able (emotionally) to empower and encourage others to walk in authority.

We need to allow the Holy Spirit to examine our own heart. Control is the opposite of humility. Psalm 147:6 reminds us that "The Lord lifts up the humble; He casts the wicked down to the ground." The Lord will honor a humble heart.

Control is also a spiritual part of witchcraft and demonology. A person who partakes in the practice of witchcraft or demonology (animism or shamanism) is a person seeking control over another person or entity. Control without boundaries can be extremely damaging. Not everyone who exhibits an ungodly controlling spirit is involved in witchcraft. But the manipulation that accompanies the spirit of control is very damaging and it builds the impression of "power" to the one exhibiting the spirit of control. People who desire "power" manipulate and use control to bring them to a point of ungodly leadership.

Control is the opposite of trust. If a person needs to be in control of everything that goes on their life, that person is not trusting God. If there is no trust in the Lord, then control is in that person's hands.

Control is a stronghold that can affect a community or government situation, not just an individual. Community includes schools, churches, or organizations that work within a community. Control is evidenced by the fear of failure. If a person believes that they must be perfect or else they will be a failure, that is out of balance self-control, which leads to a lack of trust in the Lord. That exhibits a spirit of control.

Proverbs 3:5-6 says to "Trust in the Lord with all your heart; and lean not unto your own understanding. In all your ways acknowledge Him and He will direct your paths." When we ask the Lord how to do something it means humbling ourselves. Proverbs 3:7a adds, "Be not wise in your own eyes." That is release and trust and humility all mixed in together.

- **Death**

In 1994 while in Kazakhstan, I was prayer walking and seeking insight from the Lord about how to pray for Kazakhstan. The Lord spoke to my heart and said there was a spirit of death over the country. I kept that thought in prayer. Not long after that, several people told me they had heard from the Lord there was a spirit of death over Kazakhstan as they prayed.

A spirit of death can be evidenced by physical death as well as by spiritual death. A spirit of death can also mean that the basis of the culture is one that would bring death and dying to a country economically, socially and spiritually. Jesus warned us in John 10:10 that "The thief does not come except to steal, and to kill, and to destroy. I have come that they may have life, and that they may have it more abundantly."

The enemy certainly can, and does, destroy countries. The enemy wins when an expatriate Christian worker in a cross-cultural mission has a death in their family in America. Those circumstances make it necessary for them to leave the field and the work they are doing for the Lord. Even if it is for a short time, the work is interrupted and this causes a slow down in kingdom building.

You see the enemy's strategy? Interrupted work for the kingdom! It is important that we recognize attacks and strategies of Satan so we can pray against them before they occur.

I am not encouraging anyone to blame Satan for all painful or hurtful situations; don't look for a demon around every corner. But I am encouraging you to learn about the tactics of the enemy. Read and study God's word; learn to identify when it is the enemy creating delays, disappointments or interruptions and use God's word to gain the victory over Satan.

Remind yourself and the enemy that John tells us in First John 4:4, "You are of God, little children, and have overcome them (evil spirits) because He who is in you is greater than he who is in the world."

We need to ask the Lord to make us sensitive to His purpose when unusual circumstances occur. We need to make sure we know exactly what the Holy Spirit wants us to pray in any given situation. We must always look at circumstances around us through the lens of our relationship with God. We do not look at God through the circumstances we are living in. We have victory because of His promises, His life and death and resurrection. We look to God's word and use the authority He has given us.

If we are not living a humble, obedient, Spirit-filled life, we cannot expect His power and/or authority to be active in our lives. If God has told you to go to someone and apologize and you refuse to humble yourself to that person, do not expect God to work a miracle through or for you. Disobedience is like a brick wall that blocks God's Spirit from working for, through, or in us.

If we walk in obedience, and I believe obedience is the key, we can change our neighborhood, city, state, country and the world for Christ. If we do not like what happens in our government and we ask God to change something, remember that He says in 2 Chronicles 7:14, "If my people who are called by my name will humble themselves and pray and seek my face and turn from their wicked way, I will hear from heaven and I will answer." The key is humility in our obedience to this Scripture.

- **<u>Fear</u>**

The opposite of fear is trust. Fear governs many people and situations. People are afraid of what others think of them, afraid of the dark, and afraid of what will happen in the future. God does expect us to use common sense and not put ourselves in dangerous situations, but we are not to live in fear.

If a spirit of fear comes on you at night when you go to bed or after dark, you can bind it away. Remember the blood of Jesus protects you. Say it out loud. Symbolically paint it over your doors and windows. The blood of Jesus: *nothing* can cross that line. But we must appropriate what He has given us.

1 John 4:18 says, "There is no fear in love; but perfect love casts out fear, because fear involves punishment, and the one who fears is not perfected in love."

And in Philippians 2:9-10 we are taught that "For this reason also, God highly exalted Him (Jesus) and bestowed on Him the name which is above every name, so that at the name of Jesus every knee will bow, of those who are in heaven and on earth and under the earth."

- **<u>Greed and Hoarding</u>**

The opposite of greed and hoarding is generosity and trust. In Philippians, Paul was encouraging the believers to give money, he said that it wasn't for his increase but it was for their blessing. We need to give with the attitude that we aren't giving to get back but simply to bless someone else. We can never out-give the Lord.

Hoarding of goods, whether food or supplies, is sin. Hoarding is not the same as having a normal supply of something. Hoarding is holding onto something in order to meet a possible need.

Matthew 6:25-32 teaches, "For this reason I say to you, do not worry about your life, what you will eat or what you will drink; nor about your body, what you will put on. Is not life more than food and the body more than clothing? Look at the birds of the air, for they neither sow nor reap nor gather into barns, yet your heavenly Father feeds them. Are you not of more value than they? Which of you by worrying can add one cubit to his stature? So why do you worry about clothing?"

Matthew continues, "Consider the lilies of the field, how they grow; they neither toil nor spin, and yet I say to you that even Solomon in all his glory was not arrayed like one of these. Now if God so clothes the grass of the field, which today is alive and tomorrow is thrown into the oven, will He not much more clothe you?

"O you of little faith! Therefore do not worry, saying, 'What will we eat?' or 'What will we drink?' or 'What will we wear?' For after all these things the Gentiles seek. For your heavenly Father knows that you need all these things."

People get caught in poverty and it becomes a stronghold that keeps them from maturity in Christ. It can be the basis for self-pity, fear, anger and many other strongholds. Poverty can be a crutch to which people hold onto when they are afraid to trust God and release their own will to Him. Poverty is also a result of lack of obedience to His word. Poverty often brings attention to a person who craves attention and needs to be nurtured in an ungodly manner.

Poverty is often caused by selfishness. The Bible teaches us in Malachi about giving. Malachi 3:8-12 asks, "Will a man rob God? Yet you have robbed Me! But you say, 'In what way have we robbed You?' 'In tithes and offerings. You are cursed with a curse, for you have robbed Me, even this whole nation. Bring all the tithes into the storehouse, that there may be food in My house, and try Me now in this,' says the Lord of hosts, 'If I will not open for you the windows of heaven and pour out for you such blessing that there will not be room enough to receive it. And I will rebuke the devourer for your sakes, so that he will not destroy the fruit of your ground, nor shall the vine fail to bear fruit for you in the field,' says the Lord of hosts; 'And all nations will call you blessed, for you will be a delightful land,' says the Lord of Hosts."

When we hoard our money for our own personal use we demonstrate to the Lord that He cannot trust us with more money. Everything we have comes from the Lord, whether it is cash or tangible goods. He is the giver of good to each of us, whether we belong to Him personally or not.

2 Corinthians 9:10-11 says, "Now may He who supplies seed to the sower, and bread for food, supply and multiply the seed you have sown and increase the fruits of your righteousness, while you are enriched in everything for all liberality, which causes thanksgiving through us to God."

2 Corinthians 9:6-8 also says, "But this I say: He who sows sparingly will also reap sparingly, and he who sows bountifully will also reap bountifully. So let each one give as he purposes in his heart, not grudgingly or of necessity; for God loves a cheerful giver. And God is able to make all grace abound toward you, that you, always having all sufficiency in all things, may have an abundance for every good work."

God expects us to not only give our tithe but to give offerings of many kinds, money, tangible goods, help, kindness, etc. to those who are in need. If we have what they need, we are to help meet the need.

- **Hopelessness**

Some people call hopelessness resignation. The opposite characteristics are hope, faith, and joy. If we have no faith, we are hopeless. If we do not know that the Lord can change our circumstances or situation, we are hopeless.

If we know that the Lord can change present situations, but we don't approach life with His victory and joy we have nothing, so we remain hopeless. Romans 15:13 says, "Now may the God of hope fill you with all joy and peace in believing, so that you will abound in hope by the power of the Holy Spirit."

- **Manipulation**

The opposite of manipulation is sovereignty and trust. If you or someone you know is a manipulative person, or if you get your own way by using manipulation or guilt, then you have this problem. Have you ever known anyone who said, "If you do not do this or that, I will kill myself" or, "If you won't do this, you don't love me?" Emotional manipulation is a spiritual stronghold. Bind that spirit of manipulation and ask the Holy Spirit to replace it with knowledge and understanding and a spirit of trust.

- **Pride**

The stronghold of pride has been identified in most countries. The opposite of this stronghold is humility. All wisdom and talent is given from the Lord it is not self-made. Pride is a result of not giving the Lord the credit.

Proverbs 2:1-7(a) teaches, "My son, if you receive my words, and treasure my commands within you, so that you incline your ear to wisdom, and apply your heart to understanding; yes, if you cry out for discernment, and lift up your voice for understanding, if you seek her as silver, and search for her as for hidden treasures; then you will understand the fear of the Lord, and find the knowledge of God. For the Lord gives wisdom; from His mouth comes knowledge and understanding; wisdom for the upright; He is a shield to those who walk uprightly; He guards the paths of justice, and preserves the way of His saints."

There is a spirit of pride in this country. I don't suppose that there is a country in the world that doesn't have a spirit of pride, and I don't suppose there is an individual in the world that hasn't had to deal with pride. I am talking about inappropriate pride.

The opposite spirit for pride is humility. Pride is a very dangerous and sometimes subtle stronghold. It is very hard for us to identify pride in ourselves if we are not humble before the Lord. Pride will keep prayers from being answered.

Pride takes many forms. If I think that I do something better than someone else, that is pride. If I think that I have a little more knowledge than someone else, and have judgment toward the person, that is pride. If I think I can identify what is wrong with you and have the right to tell you, that is pride.

God tells us that He gives knowledge, wisdom, and understanding. What right do we have to become prideful because we have a gift or a talent another person does not have? That should bring humility instead of pride. We should be humble because we know that the God of creation, the God of the universe, trusted us enough to give us His gifts. We should be on our face asking Him how to use what He gave us.

Additional Scriptures about pride:

Proverbs 29:23 "A man's pride will bring him low, but a humble spirit will obtain honor."

Proverbs 8:13 "The fear of the Lord is to hate evil; pride and arrogance and the evil way and the perverse mouth I hate."

Proverbs 11:2 "When pride comes, then comes shame; but with the humble is wisdom."

Proverbs 13:10 "By pride comes nothing but strife, but with the well-advised is wisdom."

Proverbs 14: 3 -4 "In the mouth of a fool is a rod of pride, but the lips of the wise will preserve them."

Proverbs 16:18 "Pride goes before destruction, and a haughty spirit before a fall."

Proverbs 21:24 "A proud and haughty man – "Scoffer" is his name; he acts with arrogant pride.

- **<u>Self-gratification</u>**

Self-gratification includes selfishness, obsessiveness, lack of self-discipline, engaging in inappropriate sexual activity, and addictions of all descriptions. The opposite spirit is total trust and faith in Christ. It is letting Christ fill the need in the emotions that you are trying to fill with the obsession.

The opposite of a sexual addiction or stronghold is chastity. Adultery, fornication, masturbation are all self-gratification. Self-gratification is selfish and disobedient. To follow Christ is to have laid aside our own desires in obedience to His instructions of how to follow Him. We lay down our own life and sacrifice our self-interests to allow Christ to raise us up to follow Him in new life.

- **<u>Self-Pity</u>**

Self-pity is very close to hopelessness. You should pray against self-pity with praise, thanksgiving and joy. Yes, life is difficult. It is difficult in every country. We all have different problems we have to address, and it is our choice how we respond in life. If we choose the path of joy, thanksgiving, and praise we are going to see our lives revolutionized.

- **<u>Unforgiveness</u>**

If we don't practice forgiveness, our prayers are hindered. Forgetful forgiveness is forgiveness that truly frees us. There is not an "if" after forgiveness. We don't forgive "if" someone else does something and apologizes, we forgive them and release the hurt and live in that freedom. We are responsible only for our own obedience, not someone else's obedience. Christ's unconditional forgiveness is the characteristic we want to replace unforgiveness.

When we forgive, we forgive from our heart and mind. It may take time to be able to forgive a wrong, ask the Lord to make you willing to forgive. Forgiveness does not mean you will forget the wrong, it means that the sting of hurt, bitterness, resentment and anger are gone.

Jesus' instruction is clear, we are forgiven as we forgive others. We have been forgiven much, so we must forgive others much. Matthew 6:14-15 says, "For if you forgive men their trespasses, your heavenly Father will also forgive you. But if you do not forgive men their trespasses, neither will your Father forgive your trespasses."

The Lord has never instructed us to do something that He has not done. He has given us the power to complete what He asks through the indwelling Holy Spirit.

9

Praise Praying

Psalms 22:3 teaches, "But You are holy, enthroned in the praises of Israel." We, the Church of Jesus Christ, are now joined together with God's chosen people the Israelites, as His Body. We do not replace the Jewish people, we join with them. As Paul explained to the church at Ephesus we are now known as "one new man" (Ephesians 2:14-18).

Praise praying is a habit we should all get into!

Psalms 100:4-5 encourages us to "Enter into His gates with thanksgiving, and into His courts with praise. Be thankful to Him, and bless His name. For the Lord is good; His mercy is everlasting, and His truth endures to all generations."

Praise breaks bondages and strongholds. Praise shows the devil that we trust the Lord with all events and circumstances in our lives and we do not live in fear. Praise tells the Lord that we believe in His sovereignty and that we trust Him with our life.

There was a period of several years when the Lord had me fast one day a week. In 1995 I was preparing for my first fast day of that year when the Lord spoke to me and said, "We are not going to have a day of fasting and prayer this year." I was surprised and asked Him, "Why, and what are we going to do?" He replied, "We will have a day of fasting and praise."

Oh, how exciting, I thought. I understood in my Spirit that He wanted me to have a full day of praising Him, thanking Him and loving on Him, and in turn I would have a full day of being in His presence. It turned out to be the most wonderful year of fasting and praising the Lord one day each week. There is something in every circumstance for which to praise the Lord.

Praising the Lord lifts burdens, removes fear, gives insight into situations, lightens any dark mood and fills our mind and spirit with joyful love. Being filled with His love and being in His presence gives Him an opportunity to speak to us about areas in our lives that He knows need some change.

The writer of Hebrews 13:15 quotes from the Psalms when he says, "Therefore by Him let us continually offer the sacrifice of praise to God, that is, the fruit of our lips, giving thanks to His name." The writer of Psalms 116:17 says, "I will offer to You the sacrifice of thanksgiving, and will call upon the name of the Lord."

There are times when giving praise and thanksgiving to the Lord is truly a sacrifice. But living in obedience to His Word is what brings us freedom. When the Lord asked me to move to Kazakhstan I wanted to live in the United States and serve Him here. I was taken by surprise when He asked me to go to Central Asia.

I had a spiritual and emotional struggle to go through in order to get to the place where I released my will and could walk freely and joyfully in His will. That was a time when giving Him praise was definitely a sacrifice. But the more I praised Him, even through tears and sorrow, the more my spirit relaxed into His will.

I did not want to leave my family and my grandchildren. My Mom and I had hoped that we would live together one day, but now I would be gone. I was fifty years old when the Lord asked me to make that move but I knew Him and I knew He would provide the way and give me His peace if I lived in obedience to His will for my life.

The sacrifice of praise often is not easy but it is necessary. Even when something hurts us, we know everything that touches us must come through His hands first.

I have a friend whose only son died suddenly in his twenties. It was a shock and a horrid loss. On the second morning after his death she was up early asking the Lord what she should do. How was she to survive this? How could she function normally again? He answered her with, "You know where to find Me." She knew immediately what He meant. As difficult as it was she put on praise music and begin to praise the Lord. She praised Him and thanked Him for being her strength. She knew from experience that the only peace she would find would be in Him. She knew He was with her but she needed to feel Him and sense Him beside her.

He relieved the death grip of pain she felt in her heart in the months to follow and He continued to give her peace and comfort. Had she not surrendered her hurt and pain to Him, she would not have healed. She gave up her right to live in self-pity and turned to Him to live in the peace and healing of Jesus.

There are times when I have prayer walks of praise. I will have already prayed over the area with petitions for salvation, healing, and neighborhood needs, and then the day comes when the Holy Spirit will suggest a praise walk. I praise Him for all He has done in each home, for the beautiful scenery, for the work He is doing in the individuals who live in the houses.

I praise Him for eyes to see as I walk and for ears to hear the birds and children playing. I praise Him for each person I walk by or see and for the businesses He is blessing as I pass by them. I praise Him for mercy for each person and for the door of eternal salvation He has opened for them. I can always find something for which to praise Him!

The joy of the Lord activated in our life will bring peace and can set the stage to change circumstances. Joy defeats the enemy because it is the result of trust. Joy puts depression to flight, replaces oppression and brings strength. Remember Nehemiah 8:10(b) promises, "For the joy of the Lord is your strength!"

When you are tired or sick, and you do not feel like praising the Lord - do it anyway! If you are obedient with your mouth, pretty soon your head, heart and spirit will pick up on what your mouth says. The joy of the Lord will fill you. It will move from your tongue forming the words, to your head, then to your heart and spirit. At that point, the way you perceive your circumstances will change and the way you react and respond to your circumstances will also change.

In 1992, a doctor told me that I had cancer. I drove home in a fog. My Mom was visiting me at the time and I did not want to upset her, but I also did not know what to do next.

I called a doctor I had worked for and gave him the name of the oncologist that the other doctor had recommended. He said that I had gotten the best oncologist in town. That brought some relief. I told my Mom what the doctor had said and we prayed, ate dinner and I went to bed. But I wanted to cover my head and hide.

We had made plans to go sightseeing the next day before Mom flew home. In the morning when I woke up, I wanted to bury myself in the covers and feel sorry for myself all day, but since we had made plans, I knew I had to get up. I told the Lord I simply did not know how to pray and He said, "Praise Me." I made a short reply of, "Oh sure." He then reminded me of First Thessalonians 5:16-18, "Rejoice always, pray without ceasing, in everything give thanks; for this is the will of God in Christ Jesus for you."

I knew the Spirit of the Lord had spoken to me, I recognized His voice. Mom and I got ready and we took off. I tried to make myself praise the Lord. I kept trying to say, "thank You" and "praise You" but it was so hard to say for these circumstances. However, I continued to practice speaking out praise and thanksgiving.

After lunch we were driving to our next stop, when I realized I could easily make my mouth say "thanks" and give the Lord praise. It was not much longer before it had changed from just my lips moving to say "thank You" to the words actually coming from my mind with a bit of joy. Soon I realized my heart was rejoicing and I was truly praising and thanking my Lord for what He was going to do through this situation.

The next morning I was getting ready to take Mom to the airport when suddenly the Holy Spirit spoke to me that "this sickness is not unto death." I called to Mom and asked her where this Scripture was. She told me it was in John 11. I quickly dressed and looked up John 11:4. Right there in red letters were the words that Jesus spoke about Lazarus and the very same words the Holy Spirit had spoken to me a few minutes before.

I knew I would be healed and I began praising the Lord!

Then I did what I knew to do. I asked others to pray and praised the Lord. Yes, they still did surgery, but the next biopsies came back negative of cancer cells. I have always wondered–had I not learned to praise the Lord and trust Him with thanksgiving, would I have been healed? We do not earn our healing any more than we earn our salvation through doing things "just right;" but humility and obedience have consequences just as disobedience and self-direction have.

Stronghold Chart

Philippians 2:5
Let this mind be in you which was also in Christ Jesus.

STRONGHOLDS	SCRIPTURE	OPPOSITE SPIRIT
Addictions		
Alcohol	Ephesians 5:18	*Be filled with the Spirit*
Drugs	Titus 2:3	*Self-control*
Sexual	Ephesians 5:3-5	
Complaining	Phil. 2:14,15,16	*Encouragement*
Confusion	I Corinthians 14:33	*Clarity, order*
Control		
Financial	Luke 18:18-25	*Release*
Life	Matthew 26:39	*Trust*
	Luke 18:29-30	*Obedience*
Death		
Spiritual death	John 10:10	*Life*
	Luke 19:1-10	
	Matthew 10:28	
	Psalm 118:17	
Physical death	John 11:1-46 - Lazarus	*Life*
	Luke 8:49-56	
(includes abortion & murder)		
Deception	Psa. 119: various verses	*Truth*
	John 8:31-32	

STRONGHOLDS	SCRIPTURE	OPPOSITE SPIRIT
Fear	I John 4:18 2 Timothy 1:7	*Trust*
Greed/Hoarding	Luke 18:18-23 I Kings 17:9-16 Philippians 4:14-20	*Generosity* *Trust*
Hopelessness	Romans 15:13 Hebrews 11:1 Ephesians 1:15-23 Ephesians 2:8-10	*Hope* *Faith* *Joy*
Intelligence	I Corinthians 2:16 Ephesians 5:15-21	*The Mind of Christ* *Wisdom*
Manipulation	Daniel 2:20-22	*Sovereignty* *Trust*
Poverty	Proverbs 13:22 Philippians 4:19 Matthew 6:25-34	*God's provision*
Pride	I John 2:16 Proverbs 16:19 I Peter 5:5(b),6 James 4:10	*Humility*
Selfishness	Philippians 2:3	*Humility, meekness*
Self-pity	Ephesians 5:19,20 Nehemiah 8:10 I Thessalonians 5:18 Hebrews 10:31-35	*Praise* *Thanksgiving* *Joy*

STRONGHOLDS	SCRIPTURE	OPPOSITE SPIRIT
Sexual Activity/Lust	Proverbs 6:32	*Chastity*
	Matthew 5:27,28	
	Romans 13:13,14	
	I Corinthians 6:12-20	
	Romans 1:18-32	
Unforgiveness	Psalms 130:4	*Forgiveness*
	Colossians 2:13	
	Luke 23:34,35	
	Matthew 6:14,15	

<u>Chastity</u>: abstaining from all or immoral (unlawful) sexual activity

<u>Spiritual Strongholds - Individual</u>
- are in our minds (double mindedness)
- can be unrepentant carnal iniquities or sins
- can be areas which we "reactivate" in particular circumstances
- are activated by allowing iniquity to produce results
- we are responsible for allowing and activating strongholds; therefore, we cannot transfer responsibility to "Satan"

<u>Stronghold Locations</u> - areas where Satan is/has been in control
- altar areas where sacrifices are made
- mosques, temples, shrines
- areas where fortune tellers, palm readers, etc. are located
- places of government authority where influential decisions are made
- areas where sin abounds (abortion clinics, orphanages, pensioners homes, drug houses, prostitution houses, etc.)

LaVergne, TN USA
30 June 2010
187968LV00002B/1/P